Faithful Servant Series
Meditations for Church Volunteers

Faithful Servant Series
Meditations for Church Volunteers

Valerie Gittings
Christopher L. Webber, Series Editor

MOREHOUSE PUBLISHING
A Continuum imprint
HARRISBURG • LONDON • NEW YORK

ABC Publishing
ANGLICAN BOOK CENTRE
TORONTO ■ CANADA

Copyright © 2003 by Valerie Gittings

Morehouse Publishing   Anglican Book Centre
P.O. Box 1321   600 Jarvis Street
Harrisburg, Pennsylvania 17105   Toronto, Ontario, Canada M4Y2J6

Cover design by Corey Kent

Library of Congress Cataloging-in-Publication Data

Gittings, Valerie.
    Meditations for church volunteers / Valerie Gittings.
        p. cm. — (Faithful servant series)
    ISBN 0-8192-1927-4 (pbk.)
    1. Lay ministry—Meditations. I. Title. II. Series.
    BV4596.C49 G58 2003
    242'.69-dc21
                                                    2002013185

Printed in the United States of America
00 01 02 03 04 05   10 9 8 7 6 5 4 3 2 1

*To my mother, who took me to the library,
and my father, who taught me to swim*

Contents

─────────── "You Were Chosen" ───────────

Were you chosen to read this book? Perhaps it was given to you in a public cere-
mony or maybe it was handed to you with a quiet "you might like to look at
this." Maybe, on the other hand, it reached out to you in a bookstore and said,
"Buy me!" Many books choose us in such ways and this book is likelier to have
done so than most. But however this book came to you, it almost certainly happened because you have also been chosen for a ministry in the church or for
church membership. Perhaps you hadn't considered this as being chosen; you
thought you decided for yourself. But no, you were chosen. God acted first, and
now you are where you are because God took that initiative.

God acts first—the Bible is very clear about that and God acts to choose us
because God loves us. And who is this God who seeks us in so many ways, who
calls us from our familiar and comfortable places and moves us into new
parishes and new roles? Christians have been seeking answers to that question
for a long time.

Part of that answer can be found within the church. We come to know God
better by serving as church members and in church ministries. God is present

with us and in others all around us as we worship and serve. But there is always more, and God never forces a way into our hearts. Rather, God waits for us to be quiet and open to a deeper relationship.

And that's what this book is about. This is not simply a book to read but to use, in the hope that you will set aside some time every day for prayer and the Bible—and for this book. So give yourself time not only to read but also to consider, to think about, to meditate on what you have read. The writers of these short meditations have been where you are, thought about their experiences deeply, and come to know God better. Our prayer is that through their words and experience and your reflection on them, you will continue to grow in knowledge and love—and faithful service—of this loving, seeking God.

— Christopher L. Webber
  Series Editor

Acknowledgments

I'd love to be able to thank, by individual name, all the dedicated church volunteers who have so enriched my life, but I'd be sure to leave someone out—and anyway this book doesn't have enough pages. So a collective thanks to members of the following congregations will have to suffice: Wayne Park Baptist Temple in Erie, Pennsylvania, where a women's group threw me a lifeline; Pughtown Baptist Church in Pughtown, Pennsylvania, where I was encouraged to become more myself; West Shore Baptist Church in Camp Hill, Pennsylvania, where older members gently offered wisdom laced through with kindness; and First Baptist Church in Fairmont, West Virginia, where people of integrity upheld Christian principles in a time of adversity, winning my everlasting admiration. Each place holds precious memories for me of wonderful people who shared their faith, shaping mine in the process.

My thanks, also, to Debra Farrington at Morehouse, who has been the soul of encouragement; to Nancy Fitzgerald, whose thoughtful suggestions I greatly appreciated; and to Chris Webber, an editor of the highest order.

And last, to my husband, Carl, who, every day, helps me understand the true meaning of salvation.

Introduction

I was raised in the church but left it in my teens, as so many of us did when our inherited, childhood faith failed to hold up under the crush of life's unkind weight. The death of my young aunt when I was in high school convinced me that God did not care about people in any way that mattered. I remained an agnostic for a long time, returning to the church, oddly enough, after the death of my first husband.

I went back because I had a sort of conversion experience then, during which I received an assurance of God's presence that is hard to describe. Anyway, I came to believe, and still do, that God is close at hand and very active in our lives. I gratefully started attending Sunday morning worship, but I never meant to get as involved in the church as I ultimately did.

I said a sloppy prayer that went something like this: "Well, God, I have really messed up this life you gave me. I don't see how anything good can come of it, so if you want it, you can have it." (Generous of me, wasn't it?) I advise anyone who'll listen not to pray such a prayer unless they really mean it. I prayed this way, and the next thing I knew, I was married to a minister. So for twenty years

I've been attending worship, teaching Sunday school, participating in women's groups, singing in the choir, organizing meals, helping with youth events, chairing committees—and giving thanks.

In *The Church-Idea*, William Huntington writes of the reality of God's church on earth and eloquently sums up many of my own feelings:

> *The divine thought [about the church], it is true, must be perfect for the very reason that it is divine. But the working out of the thought has been left, to a great degree, in the hands of [human beings]. Part of the purpose was that in this building of the Temple we should be "laborers together with God." God's share in the work has indeed been perfect; ours very far from perfect. This is why it was said that we should find cause for mortification; for is anything more mortifying, when we have the picture of what might be, and of what was meant to be, before our eyes, than to observe in what a sad and terrible way human willfulness, and human pride, and human enmity have marred and disfigured in the fulfillment the fair beauty of the promise?*

And yet, along with our mortification, we shall feel gratitude and joy, if we discover that, after all, the lines of the original painting are still traceable upon the stained and torn canvas, and that underneath the incrustations of long ages there lies the perfect outline of the Mystical Body of the Lord.[1]

My experience in the church has in fact been "very far from perfect," and—if you've been involved in the church for more than, say, five minutes—I imagine yours has been, too. But that doesn't mean it hasn't been wonderful. When I look at the church, I see all these amazing people trying to find God's will, trying to do the right thing, trying to be better. Any "mortification" I have felt has been completely outweighed by my joy in being in community with them.

And sometimes faintly, sometimes more clearly, I see that "perfect outline of the Mystical Body of the Lord." Whether you have been in the church a long time or are a relative newcomer, whether you're deeply involved or hardly involved at all, I hope these meditations, in some small way, help you to see it, too.

STAYING FOCUSED

Then the one who had received the one talent also came forward, saying, 'Master, I knew that you were a harsh man, reaping where you did not sow, and gathering where you did not scatter seed; so I was afraid, and I hid your talent in the ground."

Matthew 25:24–25

We've all learned in our history books that Admiral Robert E. Peary discovered the North Pole in 1909, but that's the cleaned-up, simplified version. At the time, quite a debate raged over who had actually gotten there first, Peary or another Arctic explorer named Frederick A. Cook. Both men laid claim to the prize, accusations flew fast and furious, congressional hearings were held, the National Geographic Society weighed in on Peary's side, and still the controversy bubbled. After all that, many people now believe that neither Peary nor Cook ever really arrived at the Pole.

Cook, a physician and self-described dreamer, went not only to the Arctic but also to the Antarctic, trudging over snow and ice, enduring sub-zero temperatures and biting winds, all before the invention of Polartec® and cell phones. Meanwhile, one of Cook's relatives, who was faithfully minding the family dairy business at home in New York, was accidentally locked in a refrigerator one day—and froze to death. Does this seem fair to you?

In the parable of the talents, we find a similar story. One slave was given five talents (each talent was roughly equivalent to fifteen years of a laborer's wage) to tend to in his master's absence. Another was given two talents, and a third, one. The first two slaves traded with their talents and earned their master even more money. The third man, though, buried his single talent, trying to play it safe. In the end it got him nothing, especially not his master's favor.

God obviously wants us to take chances in life, step out of our comfort zones, accept a little more responsibility, do things we haven't done before. As the ill-fated dairyman would be the first to tell you, not doing those things doesn't guarantee our safety. And certainly, if everyone in the church played it safe all the time, things would get pretty dull in a hurry. God always needs brave souls who will remain undaunted in the face of new and challenging situations, who don't try to avoid them but rather seek them out, trusting God to provide direction.

God has designed it so that as a church volunteer you really have nothing to lose—and everything to gain—by pushing your boundaries, expanding your horizons, investing your talents with enthusiasm and joy.

"Do not judge, and you will not be judged."

They bring Grandfather to the dinner table and put his food in front of him. Then they all sit down and eat their own meatloaf and mashed potatoes, talking and laughing with one another throughout the meal. They never once speak to the old man, never ask him a question or direct a comment at him. When dinner is over, they take Grandfather back to his place on the sofa in the living room.

If you didn't know the members of this family and you witnessed this scene, you might be inclined to think poorly of them. What kind of people are these, who ignore an old man so terribly? But if you knew them in other contexts, knew them to be loving and compassionate, you'd probably be more inclined to think there must be a reason for such behavior. In fact, Grandfather is recovering from a stroke and has difficulty swallowing. At mealtimes, he has to concentrate on what he's doing; it's dangerous for him to try to talk while he's eating. So the family includes him at the table, making their meal of foods that his weakened throat muscles can handle, sharing their stories of the day so that he can hear them—but they are careful not to tempt him to speak. They are careful because they love him and are trying to protect him.

Meditations for Church Volunteers – 5

I wonder how many times I've judged others unfairly in the church, misinterpreting their actions because I didn't have the whole picture or didn't know them well enough to understand that they were motivated by true concern. I tend to think that if I've seen something with my own eyes, I must know the truth, but that isn't necessarily so. It's often the case that something appears one way but in reality is just the opposite. Maybe the biggest reason for that is that we cannot see what's in people's hearts. Intentions are invisible.

I've seen, with my own eyes, life itself do some inexplicably cruel things. If I didn't know what I know about God, I might be inclined to judge God as cruel, too. But I know God to be loving and compassionate, and I know that God loves us. When I don't understand, it's just because I don't have the whole picture. I need to trust that God has good intentions.

"Only fear the LORD, and serve him faithfully with all your heart; for consider what great things he has done for you."

1 Samuel 12:24

"John will be here." "And we know John will attend." "We can count on John, too, of course." I kept hearing such statements when I starting volunteering around the church I belong to now. I was a little curious why people were always so certain that John would be reliable in the various roles he had. As I got to know John, I began to understand the level of his commitment.

I joined the choir, which practices every Wednesday evening, and John was always there, except for a few weeks when he had back surgery. "How long have you been singing in the choir, John?" I asked him one day. "Fifty years," he grinned. I thought he was kidding, but he continued: "I started when I was twenty-three, just after I got back from the service. It was something I knew I could do for the church, so I decided to stick with it."

During those fifty years, John was married, had two children, was widowed, was remarried, and retired from his career. The church has changed pastors a number of times, endured painful conflicts and decreased attendance, and enjoyed periods of tremendous growth. Through it all, John has remained faithful and constant in his choir participation. He has also led the grounds-keeping crew, sharing his knowledge and time freely.

There are different kinds of heroes, I guess. Some do one remarkable, courageous thing, save a life, undergo terrible suffering for justice's sake. And others are not so obvious, but in the long term are just as important for the good of the community. In a world where so many things, even relationships, are disposable, where words like *loyalty* and *steadfastness* seem so out of vogue, I find it enormously comforting—and beyond admirable—that fifty years ago a man made a commitment, and every Wednesday evening and every Sunday morning, he still faithfully lives it out.

"Go, sell what you own, and give the money to the poor, and you will have treasure in heaven; then come, follow me." When he heard this, he was shocked and went away grieving, for he had many possessions.

Mark 10:21–22

What do you suppose became of this rich man? I've always assumed that after he walked away from Jesus he felt pretty miserable, regretting his choice. Did he stay miserable, I wonder, or did he find his way back to God?

Among the Seneca Indians were medicine men who seem to have had a pretty good understanding of human psychology, even without Freud and all the attendant jargon. The medicine men knew, instinctively, that when people are not pursuing the work they love, they are prone to illness. One of the roles of the medicine men was to help the sick find ways to follow their passions. The person who needed the medicine man most was the one who could not discover "the wish of his own soul."[2]

In the church, we talk about discovering our gifts, but I like the Senecas' term better, because it conveys the idea that our gifts are part of the make-up of our souls, and that we have an innate desire (wish) for a way of life that puts our gifts to good use. Aren't the happiest people you know the ones who have found their niche in life, the place where they spend most of their time doing something they're good at and enjoy doing? I've seen any number of people discover their gifts through volunteering in church, switching careers as they figure out that they're better suited to counseling, say, than to computer programming. Watch, when the children sing, when the youth group performs a skit, when the adults go on a mission trip, and you will see people in the process of pursuing the wishes of their own souls. There's no better place than the church to do that.

When I read about the rich young man, I think surely he was looking for something, or he wouldn't have questioned Jesus in the first place. Maybe he was trying to discern the wish of his own soul. Pulled by the lure of the world, he may have walked away from a connection with the divine and a chance to be well. How often have we done that? The good news for us is the same as it was for that young man. God never gives up, never stops creating opportunities for us to learn that the wish of our own souls is the very same as God's wish for us.

"When your children ask in time to come, 'What do those stones mean to you?' then you shall tell them that the waters of the Jordan were cut off in front of the ark of the covenant of the LORD."
Joshua 4:6–7

When he came home from World War II, he didn't want to talk about his time in the army much. He married his sweetheart right away and threw himself into their new life. Their first house was a tidy little two-bedroom Cape Cod. They took good care of it; the lawn was always mowed, painting kept up, furniture dusted. In the husband's den, though, was an odd note: a lamp with no shade on it. He wouldn't let his wife cover it. "Leave it," he'd say. "It's fine the way it is."

When they moved into a larger home to accommodate their expanding family, the husband was busy with his job and most of the settling in fell to his wife. She saw her chance to get rid of the eyesore. She just didn't unpack the lamp, leaving it tucked away in a box in the basement. He never mentioned it, but a few weeks later the fixture on the light in the entrance from the garage was missing. When she questioned him about it, he confessed he had removed it. "But why?" she asked.

He hesitated, and then said, "It's because of something that happened when I was overseas. I was standing in the mess line one day. We heard mortar fire, but it seemed far away. Suddenly I was blind. I couldn't see anything but black. I told my buddy I must have been hit. He took me to the infirmary, where I found out I hadn't been wounded, but instead had dengue fever. I asked the doctor when I'd be able to see again. He said he didn't know—maybe a few days, maybe a lot longer. I was too afraid to ask him if it might be never. Anyway, I lay there on that stretcher all day and all night, and I couldn't see. The next day and night passed, too, with no change, but then the morning after that, I opened my eyes, and I could just make out the outline of a light bulb suspended from the ceiling. Slowly over the next few days, I got my sight back."

"And you never want to forget your gratitude for being able to see again," said his wife, understanding in her voice. "That's right," he said. "I'll always have a bare light bulb somewhere in my house, just to be sure I don't."

We humans have built altars and kept memorials since our very beginnings because we know our tendency to forget, to become complacent. All around the church are altars and other reminders of God's amazing goodness to us. As we go about our work, let's take time to remember.

"And no one puts new wine into old wineskins; otherwise the new wine will burst the skins and will be spilled, and the skins will be destroyed."

Luke 5:37

A friend of ours told us about driving with his elderly father on a back road through their property. A tree had fallen, its trunk rotten and limbs dry and lifeless, and crashed down onto a younger, healthy tree. The old man declared, "The weight of that dead tree is going to kill the other one." His son agreed, and said that would be too bad, really. "Well, go move it off of there! It isn't too late," the father remarked. "Okay," said the son. "I'll have to bring my chain saw and chop it up some. I'll do it just as soon as I have time." But he didn't.

Each time they drove past that spot, the father would remind his son of what needed to be done. "You're right," the younger man would say. But he still didn't take the time to save the tree. It wasn't until the day of his father's funeral, after the son had had plenty of time to think about the finality of death, that he rescued the young tree from its fate.

Volunteers are in the very best position to spot the dead trees in the church. Methods and procedures, programs and traditions have life spans. They begin, they grow, they die. When they become lifeless, if they're not removed, they'll kill what's alive around them. Part of our work is to protect what is vital in the church from stunted growth or premature demise because of dead weight.

It's hard to let go of the familiar, even when it's not of benefit anymore. Change is always difficult. But sometimes, if we don't change, we run the risk of preventing essential growth. Are you on the lookout for the old wineskins and fallen trees of useless programs?

Now there are varieties of gifts, but the same Spirit; and there are varieties of services, but the same Lord; and there are varieties of activities, but it is the same God who activates all of them in everyone.

1 Corinthians 12:4

There's an old story about a king who goes to visit another king and takes with him three hunting dogs, which he presents as a gesture of good will. The second king is very pleased, as he thoroughly enjoys hunting and spends a good deal of his time roaming his vast lands, looking for prey. Both kings are happy to live in peace and look forward to years of prosperity.

A little time goes by and the second king returns the visit, bearing gifts of his own. The first king is appropriately grateful, and they extend their peacetime pact. During the feasting in celebration of their renewed alliance, the first king asks the second how he likes the dogs he gave him earlier. The second king tells him he does not want to offend, but to be honest, he had the dogs put down. They were just terrible hunters and hadn't helped him get even one rabbit. "Oh, no!" exclaims the first king. "Those dogs were specially trained. They were for hunting lions."

It's easy to overlook the abilities of others, limiting them to roles that don't allow full use of their gifts. I sometimes find myself assuming that certain individuals aren't capable of performing given functions in the church just because they never have before. But life in the community is about growing and becoming, so I've been trying to realign my thinking: Those folks may very well be equipped to function in those positions. At the very least, they might grow into the responsibility, especially if they have support from others in the church. All of the above applies to you and me, too.

The church is a dynamic organization, with constantly shifting strengths and weaknesses. We can't afford to miss our chances to use the skills and talents— including our own—that present themselves in a never-ending sea of change. It's our job to recognize them for what they are so that we can best honor the God who gifts us all.

Living then, as every one of you does, in pure grace, it's important that you not misinterpret yourselves as people who are bringing this goodness to God. No, God brings it all to you. The only accurate way to understand ourselves is by what God is and by what he does for us, not by what we are and what we do for him.

Romans 12 (The Message)

Every now and then your kids surprise you by saying something that shows they really have been listening at church. One day when my youngest was about fourteen, I came home from work to find that he had cleaned up the kitchen—without my even asking. Delighted, I said, "Well, God bless you." He replied, "He already does, whether I clean up the kitchen or not."

I was so glad he had learned that fundamental, yet extremely difficult, lesson. We who volunteer at church profess a clear understanding that we can't earn our salvation or justify our existence—after all, we don't want to be like the Pharisees—but sometimes I think we try anyway. A few of my friends, as they've gotten older, have begun to realize that they are too driven in their professional lives because they are still trying to win their fathers' approval. We have to be careful that we don't fall into that same life pattern when it comes to working in the church.

There are a lot of motives for volunteering, and many of them are questionable. In trying to win God's (or others') approval, create an identity, exercise power, or atone for sins, for instance, we might actually further the work of the church, but ultimately we would be much more effective if we operated solely out of gratitude.

"Once a man has experienced the mercy of God in his life he will henceforth aspire only to serve," writes Dietrich Bonhoeffer in *Life Together.* "The proud throne of the judge no longer lures him; he wants to be down below with the lowly and the needy, because that is where God found him."[3]

We've all experienced the mercy of God at some point or other in our lives. I certainly have! When I recall those times of mercy and consider the fact that God blesses me whether I clean up the kitchen or not, I see myself as a recipient of the great goodness that God brings. That's when I can serve others as I should— gratefully.

So Ananias went and entered the house. He laid his hands on Saul and said, "Brother Saul, the Lord Jesus, who appeared to you on your way here, has sent me so that you may regain your sight and be filled with the Holy Spirit."

Acts 9:17

In the Acts of the Apostles, three very different men all have the same name—Ananias. One is a high priest, and one is the disciple who, along with his wife, Sapphira, kept back some of the proceeds from land they had sold instead of sharing all of it with the other disciples as they had agreed. Ananias and Sapphira both died immediately after being accused of lying to God.

The third Ananias is at the opposite end of the obedience spectrum, a man intimate enough with God to express fear at the idea of going to help Saul, having "heard from many about this man, how much evil he has done" to Jesus' followers. God tells him to go anyway, and so he does. All Ananias has to do is lay his hands on Saul and say a few words, and Saul, who was struck blind during his encounter with God on the road to Damascus, is able to see again. Saul, also known as Paul, becomes a dedicated servant of the Lord.

There are lots of people like Ananias in the church, quietly tending to God's work. They don't stand up front and preach to large crowds or donate huge sums of money to the building campaign. Rather, they stay in the background, heeding God's direction, helping others, one by one, find the Holy Spirit and regain their ability to see God's will. It's surprising how quickly a church community can become more of a social club than a spiritually minded body, more of a business than a gathering of the faithful. Ananias-people are vital to a church, because they help prevent that decline by guiding it into a close connection to the divine. They gently but effectively remind other church members of God's power and grace. Frequently, Ananias-people do not hold an office or belong to a committee, but they generously give their time to assist others in church responsibilities, and they always, always remind others to consider what it is that God really wants.

Even the great apostle Paul, who had received a message directly from the Lord, benefited from a fellow human being who laid hands on him—and so can we.

Teach me to do your will, for you are my God. Let your good spirit lead me on a level path.

Psalm 143:10

The word "volunteer" comes from the Latin *voluntas,* meaning "will." To do something voluntarily is to do it of our own will, our own choosing, not from coercion or threat or sense of guilt. When we work in the church, what we're really trying to do is line up our will to match God's. Sounds simple enough, but it's not an easy task. Our individual, human wills pull us in all kinds of directions, and some of them lead nowhere near God. We need to be vigilant and honest in our attempts to do what God wants.

Finding and doing God's will might be exhausting at times, but it isn't supposed to be impossible. When we work wholeheartedly on a ministry and gradually see that no benefit will come of it, when we find ourselves feeling unappreciated and resentful, that's when we really need to examine our goals carefully. It may be that we are trying to impose our own ideas on the church, rather than allowing God to work through us. When we refuse to recognize that church activities can easily be well-intentioned and misguided at the same time, we may unwittingly squander valuable time and energy and irreplaceable resources.

I have a friend who has a self-imposed rule that she will finish every book she starts. Sometimes when I ask her what she's reading now, she tells me, "Well, I don't like this book so I'm not reading it, and I won't let myself read anything else until I finish it, so I'm not reading anything at the moment." We can get to the same paralysis in church work, too, by insisting that we finish something just because we started it. The needed work remains undone because we are so dispirited from stubbornly tending to a dead horse. In fact, the only activity we should feel obligated to continue is one we believe to be part of a divine plan.

This isn't to say that when we are truly following God's will, we're guaranteed an easy ride on a smooth road. Actually, the work may be very difficult—but we'll have an assurance, a sense that it's important. If that's missing, it may be time to do something else.

God's will be done in the church, as it is in heaven.

STAYING BALANCED

Jesus took with him Peter and James and John, and led them up a high mountain apart, by themselves.

Mark 9:2

My husband and I climbed a mountain in New Hampshire once, with our three sons. It wasn't a very big mountain, but high enough that we had quite a sense of accomplishment when we reached the top. The trip was slow, more like a saunter than a hike, because our friend Professor Waters, who was acting as our guide, insisted on pausing along the way to point out various plants and rock formations he thought our sons might be interested in. And they were. At eighty-eight, Professor Waters was still enthusiastic about nature and was never happier than when imparting some bit of knowledge about it. His enthusiasm was contagious; the boys had a great time.

"I used to bring my art students up here," he lamented. "They just rushed—rushed up the mountain, sketched as fast as they could, and rushed back down. They didn't know where they were going when they started, they didn't know where they were when they got there, and they didn't know where they'd been when they got back A terrible waste. What good is climbing a mountain if you don't pick some blueberries and eat them and enjoy the view?"

Whenever I hear people preach about this passage in Mark, they always seem to make the point that as lovely as the mountaintop is, we have to recognize that we can't stay up there all the time, that ultimately we've got to get back to the world, get back to reality. That's true. It would be wrong to keep our heads so far up in the clouds that we didn't see what work needed to be done, what beauty was ours for the looking, at the lower elevations. But obviously Jesus thought it was important to go to the mountaintop in the first place. I know that when I haven't been up there for a while, I have a tendency to lose inspiration. So I struggle to strike a balance between retreat time, when I can transcend the physical through worship or music or art, and nose-to-the-grindstone time, when I get done what I need to. And I'm learning to pay attention to the trip up and the trip down, too, stopping occasionally to eat some blueberries and enjoy the view.

For everything there is a season, and a time for every matter under heaven.

Ecclesiastes 3:1

The first summer we lived in West Virginia, we had an emergence of cicadas, popularly known as seventeen-year locusts. One day there weren't any, and the next day there were thousands of them, coming out of the ground, climbing up on fences and shrubs where they shed their exoskeletons, their red eyes bulging and their transparent wings drying in the sun. I read later that they come out in such huge numbers to ensure that at least some of them will survive against the birds that prey on them.

The winged adults live a month or so, mating and laying eggs. Male cicadas vibrate membranes on their underside to produce courtship songs to attract females, setting up an incredible racket. During this stage, cicadas eat very little; the damage they do to plants is caused by the females slicing into the wood of shrubs and thin branches of trees to deposit their eggs. The twigs split and break, causing sections to fall and die. This "flagging" is particularly hard on young plants; older, more established trees can withstand it pretty well (although it does give the trees a very unappealing brown polka-dot look).

The adult cicadas die, and the eggs hatch after about eight weeks. The new nymphs, which are small like ants, fall to the ground and burrow down in. There they stay for the next seventeen years, maturing, feeding on root systems below the surface. At the appointed time, they all emerge again. What a life cycle! Seventeen years underground in the dark, trying to find food, and one short season in the sunlight before dying.

I pitied the poor cicadas, noisy nuisances that they were. But there was one thing I envied about them: they basically do only one thing at a time. Whether they're eating, or shedding their shells, or mating, or laying eggs, or hatching, that's all they're doing. They aren't trying to raise a family, pay the bills, take care of their parents, change the oil in the car, do the laundry and the grocery shopping—and volunteer at church, too!

Maybe I can emulate the cicadas in some small way, and learn to focus on whatever task is at hand, doing my best to accomplish it without distracting myself continuously over all the other things that need to be done too. I'll get to them in due time, and give them all the attention they deserve then.

Multi-tasking may be all the rage, but addressing each matter in its own time could keep us sane. There's a lot to be said for being as single-minded as a cicada.

And after he had dismissed the crowds, he went up the mountain by himself to pray.

Matthew 14:23

It's very telling that the very first category of the Myers-Briggs Type Indicator, one of the world's most widely used personality profiles, determines whether the subject is an extrovert or an introvert. Identifying ourselves as one or the other, understanding whether we're energized or drained by being around other people, can help us cope better with relationships in our families, at work, and at church.

"Let him who cannot be alone beware of community," writes Dietrich Bonhoeffer.[4] Even the biggest extroverts need time to recharge their batteries. People unable to "center" occasionally, unable to tolerate the quiet, may be unsettled for some reason and throw themselves into church work to avoid confronting issues that need to be dealt with. They may be accomplishing some good, but if they don't reach a point where they can stand being alone when they really need to be, eventually something ill will come of it, for themselves or for the church.

On the flip side, even true introverts need time with other people, by virtue of the fact that they're human, and humans are social animals. Bonhoeffer again:

"Let him who is not in community beware of being alone."[5] People who are unable to be in the company of God's other children, for whatever reason, are not getting all they could from their time alone with God.

Striking the right balance in any aspect of life is always difficult; balancing time spent in solitude versus time spent in community can be especially hard. A "one-size-fits-all" approach to determining how much we should participate in church activities doesn't work, because our individual needs vary so much. But sorting it out is time well spent, because finding the right blend of time alone and time with others can lead to a deeper, richer spiritual life.

For all of us make many mistakes.

James 3:2

A friend of mine has a favorite expression she uses whenever she mucks things up: "You can have a clean stable if you don't keep any oxen." So we can be tidy and have an empty stall, or we can choose to put up with a little mess and have a working farm.

We can switch this saying around and look at it from the other direction: "If you keep any oxen, you won't have a clean stable." If we do anything at all, if we teach or sing or prepare the church budget or organize a youth activity, we will—guaranteed—not do it perfectly every time. We will make mistakes. We will inadvertently step on a colleague's toes. We will have to apologize and promise ourselves to try harder and do better the next time.

Even then, when we're trying as hard as we can and doing our very best, someone inevitably will find fault with something we do, especially if we're new at it. Constructive criticism is hard enough to accept graciously, but pot-shots from people who show up only on Sunday morning can really be hard to take. It isn't a good feeling to be new at a task and uncertain of ourselves. We like proficiency, and it's only natural to want to avoid making mistakes—and especially to avoid making fools of ourselves.

We spend a lot of time and effort getting good at things—that's what being a grown-up is all about. So it's very hard to become novices again, striking out in new areas, trying to move the church forward. But that uneasy feeling goes with the territory, and we need to see it as part of the package. "Let's do something, even if it's wrong," my brother-in-law used to joke. There's a kernel of right-thinking in there, really. Much better to try, to expose ourselves to criticism, even to make a mess of things, than to sit passively waiting for ministries and programs to take shape on their own, or for important decisions to be made by default.

Whenever I start beating myself up for mistakes I make in church work, I try to remember that I'm not called to be successful, but to be faithful. I'm just not allowed to give up. That's what grace is for, that's what the Good News is: No matter how many times I miss the mark, I can always have another shot at it, another day to hit it dead on.

And he rested on the seventh day from all the work he had done.
Genesis 2:2

Migrating birds fascinate me. They travel incredible distances—up to 15,000 miles per year. A bird preparing for migration eats almost constantly, storing up fat deposits. When it flies, it uses up sugars in its blood and liver, depletes its fat deposits, and finally resorts to burning the protein in its muscles. Then it has to stop and refuel, or it will die. A migrating bird selects its route carefully, avoiding high mountain ranges and large bodies of water so that it can find stopovers if needed. It gauges its speed, too: if it flew as fast as it could, it might use up so much energy so quickly that it wouldn't be able to go the distance.

We eat so much at my church that sometimes I think we must be getting ready to migrate across the ocean! Maybe it would be better for us to imitate the birds in other ways, like choosing the right paths to get where we want to go instead of charging ahead willy-nilly. And we could learn to pace ourselves, conserving our energy so that we don't find ourselves completely spent before the job is done. Those stopovers aren't such a bad idea, either: by taking a break now and then we enable ourselves to see the task through to completion.

Even though we know downtime is important, it's easy to fall into the trap of working nonstop anyway—easy because there's always so much to do and because our society reveres activity. Somehow we've gotten the notion that time not used toward some accomplishment, especially that of making money, is wasted. Rest is for the weak and relaxation is for the lazy. These are strictly human concepts. God had a different idea.

Church work can be exhilarating, and it can be draining. When you feel fatigued, you can take a break. God will understand.

The LORD said to [Moses], "This is the land of which I swore to Abraham, to Isaac, and to Jacob, saying, 'I will give it to your descendants'; I have let you see it with your eyes, but you shall not cross over there."

Deuteronomy 34:4

The story of Moses' missing out on the Promised Land strikes a chord with many of us. We work hard to achieve goals and sometimes, in the end, we don't quite reach them. Whether it's stalling out on the climb up the corporate ladder, losing the 400-meter, or investing ourselves in a creative enterprise that fails, the pain of seeing but not actually reaching the Promised Land runs long and deep. In fact, just the fear of not making it puts some of us off. We can't bear the thought that after all our training and effort, we might win second place or make it to middle management, but we won't see the top-notch results we really desire—so we don't even try.

By the same token, many of us empathize with the mythological Sisyphus, who after angering the gods was condemned to an eternity of rolling a stone up a steep hill, only to lose control of it near the top and be forced to watch it roll clear back down to the bottom. We identify strongly with that feeling of starting over, time after time, of going back to the beginning and inching our way upward again.

The French writer Albert Camus posits that Sisyphus was generally happy in his predicament, since he was performing a challenging task most of the time.[6] Personally, I'm not so sure about that, but I do agree that honest labor is sometimes its own reward. "We spent hours and hours on that fundraiser and only made a hundred dollars," we'll complain. But when we consider how much fun we had in the process and how much better some of us got to know one another, then the project looks much more worthwhile. And talk about rolling boulders uphill, how about that youth work? It's blood, sweat, and tears all the way up the mountainside—and then the kids graduate and leave town. So what do we do? We organize another youth event, invite the younger ones to sing in the choir, plan an exciting curriculum. We keep trying.

Eventually, we figure it out: we're not going to reach the Promised Land during our lifetimes, and we're not going to get the boulder to the top of the hill—and maybe that's not such a bad thing. We'll just continue to do our work in this world, and ponder what other great work will be ours to do in the next.

STAYING CONNECTED

*Then an angel of the Lord stood before them, and the glory of the
Lord shone around them, and they were terrified. But the angel
said to them, "Do not be afraid."*

Luke 2:9–10

"Don't worry!" said my father calmly, as he stooped down to put his face next to
mine. I was three or four years old, and I was lying on my back in our front yard,
hurt and very frightened. I'd been crawling around on the porch railing and had
fallen off. "You got the wind knocked out of you. You'll be okay again in just a
little while," he reassured me. "Don't be afraid." I'd been unable to get my breath,
on the verge of panic, but I trusted him, and shortly I *was* better, just as he'd
promised.

Years later, when my son was just about the age I had been when I fell off
the porch railing, my husband died unexpectedly at the age of twenty-nine.
Stunned, I literally stumbled around the house for a few days, trying to sort it all
out, trying to take care of my child. My grandmother came to me on the second
day and, taking my hands in hers, looked me straight in the eye and said words
that were strikingly similar to those my father had spoken all those years before:
"You won't always feel the way you do right now. I promise, things will be better

in time. Don't be afraid." That night I repeated those words to my son, basing my own reassurances to him completely on trust in my grandmother's honesty and in her love for me.

Among the sweetest interactions of people at church are those involving older, more experienced members reassuring younger volunteers about the important work they want to do so well. Time after time, they'll say, "Don't worry. It'll be all right." Without that kind of encouragement, many of the new people would surely feel overwhelmed by a heavy load of responsibility. They could become discouraged if their dedicated efforts seemed not to be paying off in tangible ways, and they might feel inadequate after a glaring mistake or two. But their friends remind them of the truth of God's grace: "We'll help you get it right next time. Remember, your best effort is all God really wants. Don't worry. Don't be afraid."

Thank God for those who are willing to reach back from their places of experience to where we are—maybe lying on the ground with the wind knocked out of us—and offer assurance that all is well. And thank God for the opportunity we have to do the same for those who are coming along behind us. Someone comforts and reassures us; we comfort and reassure someone else. We may be using human voices, but we're speaking angel words.

We have gifts that differ according to the grace given to us: prophecy, in proportion to faith; ministry, in ministering; the teacher, in teaching; the exhorter, in exhortation . . .

Romans 12:6–8

A neighboring church was having a clean-up day a few years ago and discovered a bell that had been purchased by the congregation forty years earlier, just before it moved from its old location. Apparently, the plan to build a bell tower had been neglected during the chaos of the move, and the bell had rested silently in the basement of the church ever since. A man on the clean-up crew exhorted his fellow congregants to follow through with the original idea of erecting a bell tower. They listened politely, but decided not to proceed. The man bided his time until he felt he just had to try again.

Once more, he exhorted the church members to honor the commitment made by their forebears, to place and ring the bell as witness of their faith to the local community. This time, one person was moved by the exhortation and offered to donate materials and labor needed for the construction. Others responded to his lead and raised the additional money required. Several months later, on a crisp autumn Sunday morning, the bell pealed out its long-awaited praises to God, and other bells in other churches all over town joined in, acknowledging the newest voice in the chorus of worship.

Exhortation. Now there's a word you don't hear every day. I'm not sure why. It's a perfectly good word, with a perfectly good meaning. "To exhort" is to incite by argument or advice, to urge strongly. Maybe we don't like the implication that we're to remind one another to do the right thing, which is sometimes the difficult thing. And there's a connection with the concept of judgment, perhaps, that we're not comfortable with.

Included among the gifts Paul lists in Romans, exhortation doesn't get a lot of attention, but it might be more common than we think. A good sermon will exhort us to higher roads, of course, but exhortation isn't meant for preachers only. Really, anyone volunteering in the church will find times that a little exhortation is called for. It might happen in committee meetings or in small group work. The members, getting a little tired, a little lax, might start considering some shortcuts, but then someone will say, "We can do better."

And they do. Everywhere, every day, the love of Christ peals out more powerfully from churches because faithful servants use the unsung gift of exhortation.

"Lord, if another member of the church sins against me, how often should I forgive? As many as seven times?" Jesus said to him, "Not seven times, but, I tell you seventy-seven times."

Matthew 18:21–22

Years ago, while I was in the throes of yet another attempt to take off some of my excess poundage, I went on a job interview that included some unusual, psychological-type questions. One was, "If you had the power to do something that is in fact impossible, what would you choose to do?" I said the very first thing that came to mind: "Oh, I'd make it so I could eat everything I wanted without gaining any weight." The interviewer raised her eyebrows but didn't reply. I had obviously messed up.

When the interview was over, figuring I had nothing to lose, I asked her what kind of responses people usually gave to that question. "Oh," she said, "they say they'd find a cure for cancer, feed all the world's hungry, stop wars—you know, that kind of thing." Realizing my answer had sounded pretty selfish, I asked, "I don't suppose I could have what the kids call a do-over on that one, could I?" "No," was her curt response. (Surprisingly, I got the job anyway.)

I've considered that question many times since it was first posed to me. What *would* I do if I possessed some kind of supernatural force that I could bring to bear on this mortal life? Over time I've come to think that I'd leave the medical cures and world peace to someone else, and I'd institute not a do-over rule but an undo button for grown-ups, like the one on the computer that changes things back to the way they were before you made the mistake. Then if we'd say or do something hurtful, we could do more than just offer an apology that might help the offended party feel better but wouldn't take away the pain he'd already felt. We could actually go back in time and make it so that our thoughtless remark, angry comment, or cruel action had never happened. That's what I'd ask for now, after having so many regrets about hurting people.

Well, that power isn't mine and isn't going to be. I can't "take it back" when I harm someone else, because time moves forward, not backward. So my only choice is to exercise extreme caution before talking or taking action. Will my words or deeds hurt someone? Will I be sorry for what I've done in a few days, or months, or years? Christian forgiveness, especially in the church, is a wonderful thing, but how much more wonderful it would be if I'd just speak and act carefully enough to avoid needing it at all.

Then his disciples asked him what this parable meant.

Luke 8:9

About a hundred years ago, when I was very young, I attended a women's conference with friends of mine from the church. One of the speakers there told a story about an old couple who followed a ritual every night at supper. The woman would bring a loaf of fresh-baked bread to the table and place it in front of her husband. He would cut off the crust from one end and place it on her plate, and then cut a second slice for himself. Night after night, year after year, they continued this practice. Suddenly one suppertime, as her husband was putting the crust on her plate, the woman snapped and began complaining, loudly and bitterly, about his selfishness in making her take the crust and giving himself the soft, second slice—every single time. He was astonished at her reaction, coming as it did apparently out of the blue. He had another reason for being surprised at her unhappiness, too. "But the crust's the very best part!" he exclaimed. "I've always wanted you to have it."

To me, the message of the story was clear: We should be aware of how people feel about what they are giving us, so we can better appreciate the gift itself. If, for all those years, that woman had only realized that her husband was giving up his favorite part of the loaf, she surely would have thought his little daily gift was wonderful and never would have become angry with him.

Later that day, as I talked with my friend Cindy about the story, it became clear she had a completely different interpretation: "When we give a gift, we should be sure it's something the person wants and not assume that just because we like it ourselves the other person will enjoy it, too." I thought that was a pretty interesting comment, but I also thought my friend was just plain mistaken. "Why," I thought to myself, "that's not what the speaker was trying to say at all. Cindy's wrong." Which meant, of course, that I was right.

One thing I've learned in the many intervening years since first hearing the crust-of-bread anecdote is that frequently (in fact almost always) there is more than one lesson to be found in a story. A variety of interpretations serves only to make the story more valuable. To label any of them "wrong" is foolish.

In the same way, recognizing the value of different viewpoints, keeping the right spirit about the bread we receive as well as about the bread we give, serves only to make our work in the church more meaningful.

How very good and pleasant it is when kindred live together in unity!

Psalm 133:1

One of my favorite stories is about a man who was stranded alone on a desert island for a number of years. When he was finally found, his rescuers discovered, much to their amazement and puzzlement, that he had built three separate buildings. "Why three?" they asked him. "That first one," he replied, gesturing toward the primitive structures, "that's my house—where I live. The second one, that's my church—where I worship. And the third one, well, that's the church I used to go to."

Boy, if we don't find ways to divide ourselves up, even when there's only one of us! What devil is in us that we constantly disagree and separate? Jesus founded the church, and it was no time at all until its members were at odds. Church fights and denominational splits have happened much too frequently through history, over issues as large as slavery to those as small as the color of the new carpet. People don't agree, become angry because the "other side" won't get in line, and if there's no resolution, eventually some of them will leave, either to join another congregation or to quit church altogether. When members of a church in Pennsylvania had a blow-up, one of the factions bought the property on the other side of the parking lot and erected an identical building there. The issue they disagreed over has long since faded, most of the people involved are deceased, and what remains is that striking and silent brick duo, a lasting monument to a Christian community that could not get along.

We hear about divisions in the church so often that if it weren't so tragic it would be laughable. Why is it, then, that we so rarely hear of reconciliation and merger? It seems that once we split we stay split. Jesus preached unity, and in theory we all subscribe to it, but in reality we practice all manner of disunity.

People who work in the church have a responsibility to safeguard it from fracture. When we see those fault lines forming, we need to ask ourselves: Am I adding to this problem, or am I doing everything I can to help my kindred live together in unity?

But they urged him strongly, saying, "Stay with us, because it is almost evening and the day is now nearly over."

Luke 24:29

The same week that a much-loved matriarch of my church died, a retired couple who had been quite active in the church moved out of state to be near their daughters. Elizabeth, the matriarch, was highly respected for good reason. She contributed her time and skills to both the church and the community at large in very tangible ways. At her memorial service, young and old alike stood to tell of the profound difference Elizabeth had made in their lives, through her teaching and through her friendship. Marvin and Carol, the retired couple, energetic and intelligent, had worked diligently in the church in a number of capacities, lending their many talents wherever the church needed them.

Elizabeth's death and Marvin and Carol's move felt like a one-two punch to the congregation. We love them, want them with us, and sorely feel their absence. Church gatherings now that they are gone seem woefully incomplete.

When these kinds of things happen, we often feel like we need to move quickly to a resolution of our feelings, hastening to say that of course the church will survive these losses—others in the congregation are already stepping in to pick up the work. Even though that's true, and I know that eventually all will be well, I'm not ready to put on a happy face yet. The truth is, I still feel really sad. I know that God will always provide us with people who have the gifts that the church needs. I also know, though, that God made Elizabeth and Marvin and Carol distinct individuals—and all three of those unique personalities are now gone from our midst.

I've often been struck by the poignancy of this passage about the disciples on the road to Emmaus. They loved Jesus and even before they recognized who he was, they wanted him to stay with them. How dejected they must have been when he vanished from their sight! But to avoid that pain, would they have chosen never to have had the privilege of knowing him?

Beloved friends like Elizabeth and Marvin and Carol bring us great joy. Sadness when they leave is just the price we pay—willingly—for the honor of sharing part of our life journey with them.

Then suddenly a woman who had been suffering from hemorrhages for twelve years came up behind him and touched the fringe of his cloak, for she said to herself, "If I only touch his cloak, I will be made well."

Matthew 9:20–21

The Gospels are full of instances in which Jesus uses touch to make clear his absolute connection with those around him. The woman with the hemorrhage had heard of Jesus' power and was so sure of it that she believed she didn't even need to touch him directly, just brushing his clothes would be enough.

When the *Challenger* exploded in 1986, we watched the disaster being played over and over, endlessly it seemed, on television. I remember wondering whether, or at what point, the people on board realized how much trouble they were in, just how much they understood the doomed situation before they perished. What were their final thoughts? Much later, several newspapers reported that the astronauts had in fact had time to realize their fate, and that among the last recorded words were those of one saying to another, "Give me your hand." NASA disputed the reports, but it isn't hard to imagine that, in the end, the astronauts would have turned to the comfort of human touch.

After the September 11 attack, we didn't have to wonder what the victims' final thoughts were. People working in the World Trade towers, as well as the travelers on Flight 93, used what they knew to be their very last moments to make phone calls to their families and friends—to say good-bye, to say "I love you" one last time. Some of the heartbreaking messages were left on answering machines, to be kept, no doubt, as lasting testimony to precious relationships.

Interesting, isn't it, how the importance of human touch and relationships gets lost in the daily grind but becomes painfully evident when we're almost out of time? We can distract ourselves with work and possessions, but what we really want, underneath it all, is not to be alone. As we work in the church, it helps to remember that fact about ourselves—and about others. Often we hesitate to invite people to participate with us in activities, thinking they won't be interested. We don't want to "bother" them. We shouldn't hesitate to ask, though— they can always say no if they don't want to be included. Much better to risk that than to risk leaving someone alone who really needs the healing power of human connection.

Thank God for the church, where no one ever has to be alone.

"If anyone strikes you on the right cheek, turn the other also."
Matthew 5:39

Several years back, my husband and I met an older couple through our church, and they invited us to dinner at their home. After the meal, I was helping the wife with the dishes in the kitchen while the guys went to pick up some ice cream. The woman confided in me that she was unhappy in her marriage, because her husband had cheated on her, briefly, with a coworker. I told her I was very sorry to hear that and that I hoped they would be able to work things out. "How long ago was the affair?" I asked. "Shortly after we got married," she said, "thirty-seven years ago."

Confucius said, "To be wronged is nothing, unless one continues to remember it." I wouldn't go so far as to say that an affair is "nothing," but to hold on to the feeling of being wronged for thirty-seven years is certainly giving it a lot more weight than it deserves, to say nothing of wasting valuable time that could have been much happier for both of them. Anyway, you get the idea.

It's not uncommon for people who work in the church to feel slighted or unappreciated and then to harbor that feeling, usually without voicing it, for much too long. There's often a serious disconnect between the words we listen to and say in worship and the way we deal with our relationships in the church.

If someone forgets to call us, or leaves our name out of the bulletin, or changes a procedure that we've followed for years, or votes differently than we do on some issue or other, we probably shouldn't take it personally in the first place. And even if someone deliberately offends us, we can rise above our bruised egos, letting go of the sense of having been wronged.

We can realize, too, that being wronged does not give us license to abdicate our responsibilities to the church community. If everyone who has ever felt wronged quit working in the church, it wouldn't be long until there was no one left.

Living out the gospel means taking seriously the call to turn the other cheek, allowing personal feelings to take a back seat to the good of the body. It's a constant challenge, but it's a constant reward, too.

Some friends play at friendship, but a true friend sticks closer than one's nearest kin.

Proverbs 18:24

When I was undergoing tests and then surgery, I felt like God was taking care of me in a most comforting way—through the love and support of my family and friends, especially my friends at church. Because of their prayers, I continually felt a sense of peace I would never have expected to feel, and even those few times at the hospital when no one was with me, I knew that I was not alone. When I got home, my church friends brought me hot meals and flowers and books, and most important, words of encouragement. I was touched to the core by their many kindnesses, and I began to understand that being a good friend is a very spiritual matter.

Recently, I got one of those e-mail messages that have been forwarded umpteen times. It was a series of pithy sayings about friendship, like Aristotle's words: "Without friends no one would choose to live, though he had all other goods." Some of the e-mail sayings were unattributed: "A friend is someone who knows the song in your heart and can sing it back to you when you have forgotten the words," and "A real friend is one who walks in when the rest of the world walks out." Nestled there among the quotes was this simple statement: "Friends are God's way of taking care of us."

As the kids would say, "How true is *that?*" Jesus didn't leave us alone. He gave us the bread to remember him by, he gave us the Holy Spirit as our guide, and he gave us friends to share good times and bad. If we actually believe, as we say we do, that Jesus dwells in every heart, we have no choice but to take care of one another.

May God help me find all the best ways to be a true friend.

STAYING FAITHFUL

She came to him and asked, "Lord, do you not care that my sister has left me to do all the work by myself? Tell her then to help me." But the Lord answered her, "Martha, Martha, you are worried and distracted by many things; there is need of only one thing. Mary has chosen the better part, which will not be taken away from her."
Luke 10:40–42

It's probably a very good thing that I wasn't around when Martha and Jesus had their conversation about household tasks. I'm afraid I would have sounded off: "That's all well and good, Jesus. But in an hour everyone's going to be hungry, all these table linens need to be laundered, and *somebody's* got to watch the kids." For a long time, I interpreted this part of Scripture to mean that Martha's tasks weren't important in Jesus' eyes, and frankly it annoyed me. How much better, I thought, if Jesus would have said, "Oh, you're so right, Martha. Let's all pitch in and get these things done. Then we'll sit down and talk."

I've come to realize, though, that such thinking misses the point of the passage. Jesus certainly wasn't saying that Martha's tasks didn't matter; he was saying that to choose as Mary had, to refuse to be distracted by them to the point of missing invaluable time with him, was much more beneficial than accomplishing such temporal work.

We can become so immersed in the nuts and bolts, the toil and tumult of community life, that we lose sight of its true purpose. It's oh-so-easy to start seeing and doing the work for its own sake. We fix a meal at church because it needs to be fixed, we help in the office because it's time for the newsletter to go out, we go to the meeting because it's scheduled. Because these have an *indirect* impact on our spiritual lives, we can quickly forget the big picture, forget that the very reason for the work is so that the way is clear for us to choose the "better part." It's vital that we remind ourselves, over and over, of this singular fact: All of these tasks are important, but only because they enable us to remain in community, to be alive in the church, so that it can anchor us and direct and redirect us to our proper place—sitting at our Lord's feet, listening to what he says.

The daughter of Pharaoh came down to bathe at the river, while her attendants walked beside the river. She saw the basket among the reeds and sent her maid to bring it. When she opened it, she saw the child. He was crying, and she took pity on him.

Exodus 2:5–6

My friend Laura scheduled an outing for members and friends of our church to go to an artisan village in Maryland. She's organized lots of events for "fellowship" purposes, believing as she does that it's important for people in the congregation to get to know one another and to have some fun occasionally. She selected the Alpine Village this particular time because she'd been there herself and really enjoyed it. A few hours' drive from our church, it was a perfect daytrip destination. So, in her usual efficient manner, Laura made the arrangements for transportation and personally invited people well in advance of the scheduled date, Saturday, September 15, 2001. We all looked forward to another enjoyable time together.

When the day arrived, though, we were still reeling from the events of September 11, and most of us weren't very enthusiastic about the trip. After some discussion, we decided to go anyway—many of us feeling like we needed a break from the heart-wrenching reports from Ground Zero. So we met at the church, said a prayer, and piled into a couple of vans. It was a quiet ride, without so much of the usual bantering that had been the hallmark of previous outings.

At the village, we talked with a woman weaving a rug, her remarks punctuated by the steady *slap-slap* of the loom. We watched a bird carver carefully etching feathers out of wood, so lifelike we thought they would move if we breathed on them. A potter demonstrated his skill at changing lumps of sloppy clay into attractive bowls; a basket weaver showed us how she uses color to make designs in her work. We drifted in and out of the soap maker's shop, sniffing lavender and rose hips and jasmine. Every cottage we entered reminded us of another of God's wonderful gifts. Our thoughts shifted from destruction to creation, and our world, so recently and so terrifyingly out of balance, shifted back toward center.

When Pharaoh's daughter rescued Moses from the torrents of the river, she was simply taking pity on a helpless Hebrew baby. She had no way of knowing what that one act of mercy would mean in the life of God's people. When Laura scheduled our trip, she had no way of knowing that it would be anything other than a pleasant diversion. It ended up meaning so much more to us—a chance to be consoled by our friends as we struggled back to normalcy, a time to experience the nearness of God. Life in the church is full of such incidents. When we are faithful in our efforts, we often help God bring about results far beyond anything we could have imagined or foreseen.

[Jesus] watched the crowd putting money into the treasury. Many rich people put in large sums. A poor widow came and put in two small copper coins, which are worth a penny. Then he called his disciples and said to them, "Truly I tell you, this poor widow has put in more than all those who are contributing to the treasury. For all of them have contributed out of their abundance; but she out of her poverty has put in everything she had."

Mark 12:41–42

The hospital doesn't allow children on the third floor, where a young mother recuperates after surgery. She misses her two little daughters terribly. Her husband realizes that the girls miss her, too. He can see their confusion, verging on fear, when they ask over and over where she is. At the end of his visit with his wife one day, he tells her to watch out her window in one hour. He goes to his sister's house, picks up the girls, and drives them to the hospital. As they get out of the car, he points to their mother's room, and they can see her smiling at them. It isn't even close to what any of them want; what they want is to be in the very same place, to be able to touch and hug each other. But this is all the man can do, so he does it, every day, until his wife is able to come home. Years later, they all remember those very special times when, blowing kisses and waving, they sent their love back and forth across the parking lot.

Another man watches helplessly as his elderly mother grows progressively weaker from lung cancer. A lifelong voracious reader, she is too spent even to enjoy that pastime any more. Her son wants to cure her, make her young again, but of course he can't. So instead he moves her bed next to a window. Just outside, where she can see them easily, he places four birdfeeders he has built himself, and every morning he fills them as full as he can. During her final days she drowses, peacefully following the graceful motions of the cardinals and English sparrows and purple finches as they feast on the seeds. On the day of her death, the man and his family find solace in the presence of mourning doves, who softly coo a message of God's lovingkindness.

It can be incredibly frustrating working in the church. People are uncooperative or apathetic, and worthwhile projects become stymied when bickering saps the life right out of them. We see how things could be, how they really should be, and we see how far off we are. It's tempting to give in to the idea that since we can't even begin to set things right in any way that truly will make a difference, we might just as well not try at all. But the story of the widow's mite tells us exactly the opposite. However pitifully small our gifts might be, we must offer them.

We need to give what we have, do what we can, wave across the parking lot, invite the birds. And God will bless us, beyond measure.

But we have this treasure in clay jars, so that it may be made clear that this extraordinary power belongs to God and does not come from us.

2 Corinthians 4:7

When Paul wrote this line, he was referring to his own ministry, but it applies just as aptly to any church body. We have this precious community, this wonderful gift from God, contained in a fragile human organization. Paul wants us to see that contrast.

Through the ages the church has become distorted in too many ways; it has been so corrupt at times that the stench surely has reached heaven. And yet it survives—certainly not only through our efforts. All through history, the church has gotten mired in mortal woes, failing to rise to the very standards it has set for itself. Left strictly in human hands, the church would have gone the way of the dinosaur a long time ago. But it isn't solely a human institution; it is also divine. It's one of the ways God has chosen to work in the world.

In my little church, we fret over the altar cloth, argue over the type of furniture to buy for the downstairs meeting room, criticize each other in a most un-Christian way, and spend entirely too much time negotiating and cajoling. We also are incredibly faithful about visiting the sick, ministering to the bereaved, and working at the local soup kitchen. We work our hearts out for the children's programs and eagerly offer our musical talents in worship. How is this possible?

That's the point. It's all very simple and very deliberate. God uses this ever-weak, sometimes corrupt, and always beloved earthen vessel called the church to bring about astonishing goodness. That way there can be no doubt about where the power is coming from. There can be no mistaking the fact that he remains *Emmanuel,* God with us.

"I give you a new commandment, that you love one another."
John 13:34

I don't know about you, but I'm constantly disappointed by people in the church in this matter of loving one another. I expect a little more from them, I guess, since they're supposed to be practicing Christians. "Loving one another" is just the hardest thing to do, apparently, especially in the church—which is completely backward when you think about it. Too often, church folks judge each other, scramble for attention, and make mean-spirited comments. Occasionally, little bits of bigotry even pop up through the surface. Every now and then, I think I'm just not going to be able to stand it anymore, because I compare this reality with my vision of the perfect church, and it doesn't begin to measure up.

That's when I get out Deitrich Bonhoeffer's book *Life Together* and reread some of the passages that speak loudly to me. Bonhoeffer warns against "visionary dreaming; it makes the dreamer proud and pretentious." He's quite plainspoken: "He who loves his dream of community more than the Christian community itself becomes a destroyer of the latter, even though his personal intentions may be ever so honest and earnest and sacrificial."[7] Hmm. That's just how I see myself—ever so honest and earnest and sacrificial. Other people see themselves that way, too, I'll bet. Seems like that should be enough, but it isn't—especially since we run the risk of becoming proud and pretentious. That's when we start demanding our own way and judging everyone according to our personal ideals—and the church suffers.

We are not called to love the "right" idea about life in community. We are called to love the community *itself,* filled as it may be with gossips and bigots and others who disappoint us. When I think I just can't deal any more with the disillusionment that lurks all around in the church, I remember the times the disciples let Jesus down and how he still loved them. I remember, too, that I have disappointed others plenty of times, with my own set of faults, and that it's by the grace of God that my church family still loves me.

Christian community "is not an ideal which we must realize; it is rather a reality created by God in Christ in which we may participate," says Bonhoeffer.[8] It comes down simply to this: It's a privilege to be involved. And no matter how hard it may be at times, we can do no less than love the community in the same extravagant way that Jesus does.

Before all your people I will perform marvels, such as have not been performed in all the earth or in any nation; and all the people among whom you live shall see the work of the LORD; for it is an awesome thing I will do with you.

Exodus 34:10

Last year, my father had open-heart surgery, a quadruple bypass. He came through the surgery extremely well but a few days later went into respiratory arrest. He was put on a ventilator and survived—in a comatose state. After a week of being unconscious, Dad began responding to the sound of our voices. He would squeeze our hands, move his head a little. He could not walk, talk, breathe on his own, or open his eyes. His blood pressure was outrageously high, and he was receiving by intravenous lines what looked to be an entire pharmacy. Still, my father clung to life. His family and friends, his doctors, nurses, therapists, technicians, and aides had no way of knowing whether he would ever recover. Regardless, they did everything they could to keep him stabilized and give him that chance.

A few years ago, our church had a difficult decision to make. The issue was put to a vote at a special meeting, and a decision was reached by majority rule.

The following Sunday, though, a number of people, in total disagreement with the vote's outcome, were not present for worship. Over the next few weeks, they made it clear that they would not be returning. The church, deeply wounded, went into a coma, simply going through the motions of being a church. We were stricken to the core and therefore cautious. Worship was deadened, and board work became tedious and unsatisfying. Sunday morning attendance dropped, particularly among young couples with children. Still, our church clung to life. The choir members, Sunday school teachers, deacons, trustees, other volunteers, and staff, saddened as they were, had no way of knowing whether the church would ever recover. Regardless, they did everything they could to keep it stabilized and give it that chance.

Slowly, my father regained his ability to breathe, to speak, to sit up. He walked a few feeble steps with a walker, then longer distances, and now he uses only a cane. Gradually, his mind cleared and his body became stronger. Steadily, he reclaimed his old memories and his previous life. We realized he was totally well when he started talking about the future again.

Slowly, too, our church left its sickbed, at first taking a few feeble steps and gradually gaining strength to do more. Our outreach, music, mission, and children's programs flourished. One day we realized that we were no longer talking about our hurtful past but instead were working for the future.

I know the power of God. I've seen a man come from the brink of death back to abundant life. I've seen a church overcome pain and loss so completely that true joy now permeates every worship service and committee meeting. Some of the marvels God works are instantaneous and quite dramatic; others are subtle, slow-motion miracles, but miracles just the same.

For now we see in a mirror dimly, but then we will see face to face. Now I know only in part; then I will know fully, even as I have been fully known.

1 Corinthians 13:12

The ancient Celtic tradition recognizes the existence of "thin places," where the barrier between this world and the next is much less than it is everywhere else. Certain stark, particularly beautiful places, like the holy island of Lindisfarne off the coast of England, naturally make it easier to perceive God's presence. Other places, like churches and shrines, have become "thin" over the centuries because so many people have prayed there, hallowing the ground. But thin places are not limited to those sites that we have designated as sacred. For me, the Vietnam War Memorial in Washington is a very thin place, where I feel the veil between the human and the divine is less opaque than normal. The battlefields at Gettysburg have the same effect on me, and so does a conference center where I've attended a number of women's meetings.

There are thin moments, too: when a baby is born, or when someone nears death, or when an individual puts another person first, even to the point of extreme sacrifice. At those times, many experience a sensation of God as immanent.

If you look back over your life, you may be able to identify some thin places and moments. It's good to take the time to revisit consecrated ground and remember holy moments—it reminds us that an eternal God abides with us and helps us resist the temptation to experience the world strictly in temporal terms.

One of the great joys of working in a genuinely Christian community is being able to rely on the dependable "thinness" of the sanctuary. Immediately upon entering, we feel a change—the air is different, the sounds and smells not like the rest of the world. During either solitary prayer times or group worship, our thoughts focus on God much more intensely and easily than elsewhere. And sometimes in that thin place of the sanctuary, we receive the most wonderful blessing—a thin moment, of heart-changing preaching or music that transports us to the edge of another realm. Such moments in such places sustain us for the challenges we face.

Then the LORD said to Moses, "I am going to rain bread from heaven for you, and each day the people shall go out and gather enough for that day."

Exodus 16:4

My friend was describing a terrible time she and her husband had gone through when he became very ill and needed emergency surgery. The immediate outcome was not as good as they had hoped it would be, and the next several months were spent in an agony of waiting to see how well his body would heal. As she talked about how they managed to chart their way through those rough seas, she said they had learned to stay in the moment, and not to get ahead of themselves. "We just had to keep telling each other: This is where we are now. This is what's happening right now, and we don't know what's going to happen next. We just have to wait and see."

I didn't really understand what she meant until I had to go through surgery myself and wait for pathology reports to know where I stood. Then her words made perfect sense. I found myself jumping to conclusions, jumping ahead in time. I would have to repeat to myself: "This is where I am now, not down the road a few months, but right here." During that time I learned a basic life truth: It's awfully hard to wait and see.

In the church we never want to wait and see. We want to know how it's all going to come out. If we start this ministry, will it really make a difference to people? If we build this new wing, will it be used effectively? If we hire another staff person, will our programs be improved? We like to do "studies" and "analyses," euphemisms for "ways to find out what we want to know."

The story of the manna in the wilderness illustrates how God provides our physical needs, and it challenges us to trust God to give us just what we need just when we need it. Perhaps the manna symbolizes knowledge, too. We want to store up knowledge in advance the same way the Hebrews wanted to store up food in case of shortage. But God's idea, apparently, is that we get to know just what we need to know just when we need to know it, and no sooner, but no later, either. We have to trust that just as God sent manna to the Hebrews, God will send us the knowledge we need—morning by morning.

He entered the temple and began to drive out those who were selling and those who were buying in the temple, and he overturned the tables of the moneychangers and the seats of those who sold doves.
Mark 11:15

The church is a very human institution, as we know, and therefore it isn't perfect. No matter, perfection is our standard—we do what we can to achieve it.

When there's something wrong in the church, though, it's hard to know just what to do. It's always important to proceed cautiously, allowing for the possibility that emotions are clouding our perception. Maybe what we're feeling isn't righteous indignation but repressed resentment. Maybe we're being unduly judgmental. Those are valid concerns, but some things are simply unacceptable and cannot be permitted under any circumstances: physical, verbal, or emotional abuse, fiduciary misconduct, theft or disrespect of property, and so on. And as much as we don't like conflict, and don't want to set ourselves up as judges, if we see something that isn't right, we have a moral obligation to do something about it.

We don't like to talk about these things because we don't want people outside the four walls to base their opinions of the church universal on aberrant behavior. But not talking about something doesn't make it go away, and pretending there's not a problem when there really is one is absolutely the worst thing to do. Denial is dangerous, and the cost of deferring conflict is too great. Witness the additional grief caused by the failure of the Roman Catholic Church hierarchy to deal appropriately with pedophilic priests.

Jesus didn't avoid looking at the moneychangers and then later say that he "didn't really notice what was going on." He didn't tell himself that they "really weren't that bad, and anyway maybe they'll be gone next week." He didn't say, "Well, I certainly don't approve, but I don't want to rock the boat." And he didn't discuss it at a committee meeting and then decide to wait and discuss it again at next month's committee meeting. He took action.

When there's a real problem in the church, we do best to draw on every fiber of Christianity we have to solve it. And although we may struggle to decide just which tables need to be overturned, there's one thing we can be sure of—waiting will only make things worse.

The spirit of the Lord GOD is upon me, because the LORD has anointed me; he has sent me to bring good news to the oppressed.
Isaiah 61:1

"If it isn't good, and it isn't news, then it isn't the gospel," the bromide goes. But how can something two thousand years old be news?

When Flight 93 crashed in Somerset County in Pennsylvania on September 11, 2001, it looked like the bad guys had won. But then we learned that the quick-witted passengers on board had bravely thwarted the terrorists' plot to inflict an even greater evil.

Ten months later, within miles of the crash site, nine miners accidentally bored into an adjacent mine that had filled with water, which rapidly flooded in and blocked their way out. They were trapped deep under ground while rescuers frantically worked first to put an airshaft down to them and then to drill another shaft large enough to send down a cage that could lift them out. It took three days. Three days, during which the rescuers had no way of knowing whether the men had survived. Three days, during which the miners tied themselves together so none would float away, huddled together for warmth, and kept up one another's spirits. And then, finally, the good news. The rescuers had made contact with the miners; the miners were all alive; the first miner was brought out of the shaft, then the second, and so on until all nine were above ground, being reunited with their loved ones. "Miner Miracle!" read the headlines. Indeed. It wasn't just that the men were saved. Ever so powerfully we were reminded of the value, the beauty, the miracle of all human life. We saw anew the incredible gifts God has bestowed upon us, and for a little while at least, we took them much less for granted.

It seemed that in a way God was redeeming the ground of Somerset County, redeeming it with an abundance of good news. Yes, a terrible tragedy had struck there, grieving innocent families of innocent victims, but even in the ashes of that tragedy we had discovered the noblest form of self-sacrifice. And now the entire world had been able to watch altruism triumph as, on that very same ground, people from all over the country melded their expertise, their technology, and their brute strength into a relentless tool to save their brothers from peril.

God is at work in the world and in the church—now, in this present day. The gospel is news because it manifests in a fresh application in every new circumstance. And as we struggle through sorrow and strife, we can rest assured that the Good News is the eternal news. God will forever be at work.

Endnotes

1. William Reed Huntington, *The Church-Idea: An Essay Towards Unity* (Harrisburg, Pa.: Morehouse Publishing, 2002), 32–33.

2. David Swatzler, *A Friend Among the Senecas: The Quaker Mission to Cornplanter's People* (Mechanicsburg, Pa.: Stackpole Books, 2000), 36.

3. Dietrich Bonhoeffer, *Life Together* (New York: Harper & Row, 1954), 94.

4. Ibid., 78.

5. Ibid.

6. Albert Camus, *The Myth of Sisyphus and Other Essays* (New York: Vintage Books, 1955), 90.

7. Bonhoeffer, *Life Together,* 27.

8. Ibid., 30.